The Sabbath Practice

A Four-Session Companion Guide to Help You Stop, Rest, Delight, and Worship

WaterBrook

John Mark Comer and Practicing the Way

A WaterBrook Trade Paperback Original

Published in the United States by WaterBrook, an imprint of Random House, a division of Penguin Random House LLC.

WATERBROOK and colophon are registered trademarks of Penguin Random House LLC.

Published in association with Yates & Yates, yates2.com.

Originally self-published by Practicing the Way (practicingtheway.org) in 2024.

All photos courtesy of Practicing the Way.

Trade Paperback ISBN 978-0-593-60325-3
Ebook ISBN 978-0-593-60326-0

Printed in the United States of America on acid-free paper

waterbrookmultnomah.com

1st Printing

Book and cover design by Practicing the Way

For details on special quantity discounts for bulk purchases, contact specialmarketscms@penguinrandomhouse.com.

Contents

Welcome

Welcome to the Sabbath Practice. We are so happy to have you along for this four-session journey into what Jesus called "rest for your souls."* Few things are as desperately needed today as the recovery of the ancient practice of Sabbath—a full day every week set aside to stop, rest, delight, and worship.

Following this Practice has the potential to be a before/after moment in your spiritual journey, but it will not be easy. Sabbath is radical and countercultural; yet at the same time, its raw power to open us up to transformation cannot be overemphasized.

Are you ready? This Practice will be difficult, counterintuitive, and awkward to master, but it will also feel restful and deeply right. Over time it will help you become at ease in your own body.

_____

* Matthew 11v29.

As with all the Practices, we don't sabbath because it's good for us (though it is), but because we are apprentices of Jesus, our Rabbi and Lord. To follow after Jesus is to adopt his overall lifestyle as our own and arrange our daily lives around his presence and peace, or what the ancients called "following the Way." And Jesus sabbathed. In fact, many Jesus stories in the Gospels take place on the Sabbath, especially the stories of healing and deliverance. One likely reason is that *the Sabbath is a day for healing and freedom*. It's a day where the kingdom to come *has* come and we get to enter a whole new dimension of time and space.

So as you give yourself to this Sabbath Practice, remember all of this is an attempt to give ourselves more deeply to Jesus himself and let him do what no Practice or teaching or book or podcast or technique can possibly do— give rest to our souls.

Learn
about the way of Jesus

IN COMMUNITY

Process
Together
what is coming up
for you through your
experience.

WEEKLY RHYTHM

Practice
with spiritual
exercises using your
Companion Guide.

ON YOUR OWN

Reflect
on your experience with God.

How to use the Companion Guide

01 **Learn:** Gather together as a community for an interactive experience of learning about the Way of Jesus through teaching, storytelling, and discussion. Bring your Guide to the session and follow along.

02 **Practice:** On your own, before the next session, go and "put it into practice," as Jesus himself said.* We will provide weekly spiritual disciplines and spiritual exercises, as well as recommended resources to go deeper.

03 **Reflect:** Reflection is key to spiritual formation. After your practice and before the next session, set aside 10–15 minutes

---

* Philippians 4v9.

to reflect on your experience. Reflection questions are included in this Guide at the end of each session.

04 **Process together:** When you come back together, begin by sharing your reflections with your group. This moment is crucial, because we need each other to process our lives before God and make sense of our stories. If you are meeting in a larger group, you will need to break into smaller subgroups for this conversation so everyone has a chance to share.

Tips on Beginning a New Practice

It's essential to remember that all of the Practices are a *means to an end*.

The end goal of Sabbath is not to say, "I practice Sabbath." It's to apprentice under Jesus to become a person who is marked by an inner spirit of restfulness and who is calm, at ease in your own body, unhurried, kind, and present. You will become aware of what God is doing around you, sincerely grateful, emotionally healthy, and delighted by the goodness of your life with God. You will be like a rock in a sea of chaos, unmoved by the overwork, overconsumption, and overactivity of our host culture.

Because it's so easy to lose sight of the end goal of a Practice, on the following pages you'll find a few tips to keep in mind as you sabbath.

01 Start small

Start where you are, not where you "should" be. If a full 24 hours is too much, start with a half day; if that's too much, start with a few hours.

02 Think subtraction, not addition

Please do not "add" Sabbath into your already overbusy, overfull life. Think: *What can I cut out?* A weekend sports event? A house project? Weekend emails? Formation is about less, not more.

03 You get out what you put in

If you merely dabble with this Practice or take shortcuts in order to do the bare minimum, you shouldn't expect it to be particularly transformative. However, the more fully you give yourself to this Practice, the more life-changing it will be. This Practice leads to a fuller, deeper life only if you commit to it.

04 Remember the J curve

Experts on learning tell us that whenever we set out to master a new skill, our ability tends to follow a J-shaped curve: We usually get worse before we get better. If you currently enjoy your Sunday routine or day off, don't be surprised if your first few Sabbaths are awkward and difficult. Just stay with the Practice; you will come around.

05 There is no formation without repetition

Spiritual formation is slow, deep, cumulative work that takes years, not weeks. The goal of this four-session experience is just to get you started on a journey of a lifetime. Upon completion of this Practice, you will have a map for the journey ahead and hopefully some possible companions for the Way. But what you do next is up to you.

Before You Begin

A note about the Reach Exercises

We recognize that we're all at different stages of discipleship and seasons of life. To that end, we've added a Reach Exercise to each of the four sessions. In it you'll find extra exercises designed for those of you who have both the desire and the capacity to maximize your Sabbath experience. Additionally, we have suggested weekly reading and podcast episodes to enhance all four sessions. Enjoy!

A note about the recommended reading

Reading a book alongside the Practice can greatly enhance your understanding and enjoyment of Sabbath. And on the Sabbath, we actually have time to read! You may love to read, or you may not. For that reason, it's recommended but not required.

Our companion book for the Sabbath Practice is *Sabbath* by Dr. Dan Allender, who is a psychologist, author, and founder of the Allender Center in Seattle, Washington.

The Spiritual Health Reflection

One final note: Before you begin Session 01, please set aside 20–30 minutes and take the Spiritual Health Reflection. This is a self-assessment we developed in partnership with pastors and leading experts in spiritual formation. It's designed to help you reflect on the health of your soul in order to better name Jesus' invitations to you as you follow the Way.

You can come back to the Spiritual Health Reflection as often as you'd like (we recommend one to two times a year) to chart your growth and continue to move forward on your spiritual journey.

To access the Spiritual Health Reflection, visit practicingtheway.org/reflection and create an account. Answer the prompt questions slowly and prayerfully.

Spiritual Health Reflection

Part 2: Reflection (14 / 40)

I am becoming more honest and transparent with myself, God, and others

DISAGREE   AGREE

CANCEL   PAUSE   SHOW NOTEPAD   PREVIOUS   NEXT

May the God of
rest fill you with
his peace and
presence as you
rest in him.

Stop

SESSION 01

Overview

In Session 01 we explore the first movement of Sabbath and the most literal meaning of the Hebrew verb *shabbat*—"to stop." To sabbath is, at its most basic, to *stop,* to cease, to be done.

Peruse any popular magazine and pay close attention to the advertisements—a couple lounging in bed and reading the paper, a woman and her dog napping on the couch, a group of friends on the beach for a picnic. They are all images of stopping. Marketing departments the world over know that you crave a life with Sabbath, or what Marva Dawn called a "Sabbath spirituality"—a life with moments of peace, ease, calm.* And they are offering to sell you Sabbath. The irony is you don't need to buy anything to sabbath; you just need to stop.

In the Genesis story, the Creator God himself rested on the seventh day, and in doing so he built a rhythm into the fabric of creation. For six days we work and labor and wrestle with the earth, but on the seventh day, we stop. We breathe. We come to rest.

When we live in alignment with this ancient, primal rhythm, as Jesus did, we find what Jesus called "rest for your souls."** But when we fight or chafe against or attempt to outsmart this innate bodily cadence, we fracture our souls' wholeness into a million pieces. Exhaustion, confusion, alienation from God and others, harm to the earth and the poor, and even spiritual death are all the toxic waste of a life without Sabbath.

In Session 01, we experiment with Sabbath as a day to stop.

_____

* Marva J. Dawn, *Keeping the Sabbath Wholly* (Grand Rapids, Mich.: Eerdmans, 1989), xiii.

** Matthew 11v29.

Opening Questions

When instructed, pause the video for a few minutes to discuss in small groups:

01   What's your current understanding of the Sabbath?

02   Is the Sabbath a part of your life currently or not?

03   What thoughts and feelings do you have going into this Sabbath Practice?

Notes

As you watch the teaching as a group, feel free to use this page for notes.

What are some main ideas? Or what really resonates with you?

Discussion Questions

Now it's time to pause the video to reflect on the teaching. Circle up in triads (groups of three) and discuss the following questions:

01   What stuck out to you from that teaching? Was there a Scripture or thought that especially resonated with you?

02   Is Sabbath a part of your current life rhythm or not?

03   What are the obstacles that get in the way of your practicing Sabbath, either practically or emotionally?

Practice

01   Pick a time to sabbath, and give it a try

There are three basic options:

01   The Christian Sabbath on Sunday, which is best for most of us
     since it's also our day of worship

02   The traditional Sabbath from sundown on Friday night to the
     same time on Saturday

03   The midweek Sabbath for those with nontraditional
     work schedules

In biblical theology, the day begins at sundown, not sunrise as in the
modern mindset. By the end of the week, many of us are too exhausted
to really enjoy our Sabbath. For that reason, we recommend you begin
at night, if at all possible. Start with a Sabbath meal with your community
(more on that in Session 03), or simply light a candle and say a short prayer
before you fall asleep.

If an entire day is too much for you, that's fine. Start where you are. We
recommend you set aside a three- or four-hour time period, either after
church on Sunday or on a weekend night, turn off your phone, and
just *stop*.

If at all possible, get into a rhythm with Sabbath on the same day each
week. Your body will "memorize" the day, begin to anticipate it in the days
before, and live off its energy and joy in the days after.

Circle or write what you feel led to try.

_____

_____

_____

_____

_____

_____

_____

_____

_____

_____

_____

_____

_____

_____

02 Pick beginning and ending rituals

In a traditional Sabbath ceremony, called the *Kiddush,* you begin by lighting candles, praying, and eating a Sabbath meal with your family and community. And you end by praying and sharing the highlight of your Sabbath.

You can do exactly that, you can let Sunday worship with your church mark the start, or you can get creative—start with a picnic, bonfire, or hot bath. Let your creativity guide you.

Feel free to use the companion volume *Sabbath Meditations* from Practicing the Way.

What rituals would you like to try?

03 Pick one to three Sabbath activities to enter into the spirit of Sabbath

If you read the wider Sabbath literature, some of which is as old as the New Testament itself, you discover there are 12 common activities that fill up a traditional Sabbath.

01   Lighting the candles

02   Blessing the children

03   Eating a Sabbath meal

04   Expressing gratitude

05   Singing

06   Worshipping with your church

07   Walking

08   Napping

09   Making love to your spouse

10   Reading, especially Scripture

11   Spending time alone with God

12   Spending time with family and friends in conversation and celebration

This is not a to-do list, but more like 12 best practices that you are invited to grow into over time as your heart desires.

For Session 01, pick one to three that your heart is drawn to and sound appealing to your personality and stage of life. And just see what happens.

Circle or write what you'd like to do.

_____
_____
_____
_____
_____
_____
_____
_____
_____
_____
_____
_____
_____
_____
_____
_____
_____
_____
_____
_____
_____
_____
_____
_____
_____
_____

Reach Exercise

SESSION 01: STOP

We all learn differently. Some of us prefer reading, others listening, and others doing. If you'd like to go deeper, choose what resonates with you and give it a try! Even if you don't try a Reach Exercise, remember to journal in the Sabbath Reflection section on pages 36–37 before your next session as a group.

Reading

Read the introduction and Chapter 01 of *Sabbath* by Dan Allender (pp. 1–32).

Podcast

Listen to Episode 01 of the Sabbath series from the *Rule of Life* podcast by Practicing the Way.

Exercise: Sleep

Sleep a full eight to nine hours every night for an entire week. Leading research from doctors and neuroscientists like Dr. Matthew Walker in his book *Why We Sleep* has documented a growing body of evidence that dramatically highlights the crucial role of sleep in our overall health and well-being. Contrary to popular opinion, the overwhelming majority of people need a full seven to nine hours of sleep every night. Mental illness, anxiety, depression, ADHD, diabetes, high blood pressure, obesity, and even cancer have all been tied to insufficient sleep. For many of us, the first step toward becoming a person of love in Christ is learning to sleep a full eight hours every night.

See additional tips starting on page 30.

NOTES

Here are 13 tips for getting a better night's sleep, from a study by the National Institutes of Health.

01 Stick to a sleep schedule

Go to bed and wake up at the same time each day. As creatures of habit, people have a hard time adjusting to changes in sleep patterns. Sleeping later on weekends won't fully make up for a lack of sleep during the week and will make it harder to wake up early on Monday morning.

02 Exercise is great, but not too late in the day

Try to exercise at least 30 minutes on most days but not later than two to three hours before your bedtime.

03 Avoid caffeine and nicotine

Coffee, colas, certain teas, and chocolate contain the stimulant caffeine, and its effects can take as long as eight hours to wear off fully. Therefore, a cup of coffee in the late afternoon can make it hard for you to fall asleep at night. Nicotine is also a stimulant, often causing smokers to sleep only very lightly. In addition, smokers often wake up too early in the morning because of nicotine withdrawal.

04 Avoid alcoholic drinks before bed

Having a "nightcap" or alcoholic beverage before sleep may help you relax, but heavy use robs you of deep sleep and REM sleep, keeping you in the lighter stages of sleep. Heavy alcohol ingestion also may contribute to impairment in breathing at night. You also tend to wake up in the middle of the night when the effects of the alcohol have worn off.

05 Avoid large meals and beverages late at night

A light snack is okay, but a large meal can cause indigestion that interferes with sleep. Drinking too many fluids at night can cause frequent awakenings to urinate.

06 If possible, avoid medicines that delay or disrupt your sleep

Some commonly prescribed heart, blood pressure, or asthma medications, as well as some over-the-counter and herbal remedies for coughs, colds, or allergies, can disrupt sleep patterns. If you have trouble sleeping, talk to your healthcare provider or pharmacist to see whether any drugs you're taking might be contributing to your insomnia and ask whether they can be taken at other times during the day or early in the evening.

07 Don't take naps after 3 p.m.

Naps can help make up for lost sleep, but late afternoon naps can make it harder to fall asleep at night.

08 Relax before bed

Don't overschedule your day so that no time is left for unwinding. A relaxing activity, such as reading or listening to music, should be part of your bedtime ritual.

09 Take a hot bath before bed

The drop in body temperature after getting out of the bath may help you feel sleepy, and the bath can help you relax and slow down so you're more ready to sleep.

10 Have a good sleeping environment

Get rid of anything in your bedroom that might distract you from sleep, such as noises, bright lights, an uncomfortable bed, or warm temperatures. You sleep better if the temperature in the room is kept on the cool side. A TV, cell phone, or computer in the bedroom can be a distraction and deprive you of needed sleep. Having a comfortable mattress and pillow can help promote a good night's sleep. Individuals who have insomnia often watch the clock. Turn the clock's face out of view so you don't worry about the time while trying to fall asleep.

11   Have the right sunlight exposure

Daylight is key to regulating daily sleep patterns. Try to get outside in natural sunlight for at least 30 minutes each day. If possible, wake up with the sun or use very bright lights in the morning. Sleep experts recommend that if you have problems falling asleep, you should get an hour of exposure to morning sunlight and turn down the lights before bedtime.

12   Don't lie in bed awake

If you find yourself still awake after staying in bed for more than 20 minutes, or if you are starting to feel worried, get up and do some relaxing activity until you feel sleepy. The anxiety of not being able to sleep can make it harder to fall asleep.

13   See a health professional if you continue to have trouble sleeping

If you consistently find it difficult to fall or stay asleep and/or feel tired or not well rested during the day despite spending enough time in bed at night, you may have a sleep disorder. Your family healthcare provider or a sleep specialist should be able to help you, and it is important to rule out other health or emotional problems that may be disturbing your sleep.

Source: "Tips for Getting a Good Night's Sleep" in *Your Guide to Healthy Sleep*, National Heart, Lung, and Blood Institute; National Institutes of Health; U.S. Department of Health and Human Services, NIH Publication No. 11-5271, originally printed November 2005, revised August 2011, www.nhlbi.nih.gov/files/docs/public/sleep/healthy_sleep.pdf.

Sabbath Reflection

SESSION 01: STOP

Reflection is a key component in our spiritual formation.

Millennia ago, King David prayed in Psalm 139v23–24:

> Search me, God, and know my heart;
> test me and know my anxious thoughts.
> See if there is any offensive way in me,
> and lead me in the way everlasting.

South African professor Trevor Hudson has quoted one of his pastoral supervisors as saying, "We do not learn from experience; we learn from reflection upon experience."*

If you want to get the most out of this Practice, you need to do it and then *reflect* on it.

---

* Trevor Hudson, *A Mile in My Shoes: Cultivating Compassion* (Nashville, Tenn.: Upper Room Books, 2005), 57.

In between your Sabbath and your next time together with the group for Session 02, take 10 minutes to journal your answers to the following three questions.

Note: Be as specific as possible as you write. Bullet points are fine, but if you write your insights out in narrative form, your brain will be able to process them in a more lasting way.

01   Where did I feel resistance?

02   Where did I feel delight?

03   Where did I most experience God's nearness?

Rest

SESSION 02

Overview

In Session 02 we explore the second movement of Sabbath—to rest. The idea of rest sounds wonderful, but in reality, rest is a radical, countercultural act of resistance to the powers and principalities of a world at war with God and his kingdom of peace. To practice Sabbath is to draw a line in the sand against all external (and internal) forces that would encroach upon your apprenticeship to Jesus and formation into his image. It's to say, "This far you shall go, but no further." It is to defy some of the most powerful forces known to humanity as an act of non-cooperation done in love for community, for the poor, for the earth, and ultimately for God himself.

Notes

As you watch the teaching as a group, feel free to use this page for notes. What are some main ideas? Or what really resonates with you?

Discussion Questions

Now it's time to pause the video to reflect on the teaching. Circle up in your small group and have a conversation about the following questions:

01   Where are you most tired? Physically? Mentally? Emotionally? Spiritually? What is the greatest drain on your energies?

02   What is the strongest force of resistance in your life (external or internal) that attempts to keep you from Sabbath rest?

03   What are the hardest things for you to say *no* to on the Sabbath?

Practice

SESSION 02: REST

Information alone does not produce transformation. To grow, let's put this teaching into practice. Consider how the Spirit is inviting you to engage in this Practice before the next session in response to what you've learned.

All four sessions of the Sabbath Practice build on each other. Last session you set a time to Sabbath, you chose beginning and ending rituals, and you gave yourself to a few Sabbath activities. This session, we have three new exercises for you to add.

01   Prepare for the day

In the New Testament, the day before the Sabbath is called "the Preparation Day." And you really need a few hours, if not a day, to prep. Sabbath will not just happen; it's too countercultural. If you let the inertia of the day carry you, you will get sucked right back into Egypt's current.

So this session's first exercise, which will be easy for some and harder for others, is to set aside a little time, either the night before or the afternoon leading up to Sabbath, and prepare.

Here are a few recommendations:

- Go grocery shopping and stock your pantry and fridge.
- Prep your meals.
- Clean or tidy your home or apartment.
- Run any errands or pay any bills that need to be sorted before you can rest.
- Answer all your texts and emails in order to power off your devices.
- Make plans to meet your family or community on the Sabbath.
- Plan out some fun activities for play and delight.

You can do a little or a lot; it's all up to you.

Circle or write how you will prepare.

02 Prepare for external resistance

With this simple exercise, pick one to three cultural forces to say *no* to on the Sabbath.

- Phone
- Social media
- The internet
- TV and entertainment
- Shopping
- Social obligations
- Sports
- Weekend work
- Chores
- Errands
- People

It's your choice; identify a few anti-rest forces you will intentionally resist.

Circle or write what stands out to you.

_____

_____

_____

_____

_____

_____

_____

_____

_____

_____

_____

_____

_____

_____

_____

_____

_____

_____

_____

_____

03 Prepare for internal resistance

The following is a simple journaling exercise for you to complete during your upcoming Sabbath.

Find a quiet, distraction-free place and make time to breathe and come to rest in God. Then follow these prayer prompts:

01   Invite the Holy Spirit to come and illuminate your mind.

02   Then ask these two simple questions:

01 — What am I feeling today?

Here is a list of feeling words to help:

Happy	Sad	Angry	Scared	Confused
Admired	Alienated	Abused	Afraid	Ambivalent
Alive	Ashamed	Aggravated	Alarmed	Awkward
Appreciated	Burdened	Agitated	Anxious	Baffled
Assured	Condemned	Anguished	Appalled	Bewildered
Cheerful	Crushed	Annoyed	Apprehensive	Bothered
Confident	Defeated	Betrayed	Awed	Constricted
Content	Dejected	Cheated	Concerned	Directionless
Delighted	Demoralized	Coerced	Defensive	Disorganized
Determined	Depressed	Controlled	Desperate	Distracted
Ecstatic	Deserted	Deceived	Doubtful	Doubtful
Elated	Despised	Disgusted	Fearful	Flustered
Encouraged	Devastated	Dismayed	Frantic	Foggy
Energized	Disappointed	Displeased	Full of dread	Hesitant
Enthusiastic	Discarded	Dominated	Guarded	Immobilized
Excited	Discouraged	Enraged	Horrified	Misunderstood
Exuberant	Disgraced	Exasperated	Impatient	Perplexed
Flattered	Disheartened	Exploited	Insecure	Puzzled
Fortunate	Disillusioned	Frustrated	Intimidated	Stagnant
Fulfilled	Dismal	Fuming	Nervous	Surprised

Source: "Feelings Word List" from *Overcoming Depression: Workbook* by Mark Gilson, Arthur Freeman, M. Jane Yates, and Sharon Morgillo Freeman, copyright © 2009 by Oxford University Press, Inc. Reprinted by permission of Oxford University Press through PLSclear.

02 — What attachment is *under* that feeling?

An attachment is an emotional state of clinging to something we believe we need to be happy and safe. For example, you may be feeling anxiety over a relational conflict with your extended family because you are attached to their approval or opinion. Or you may be feeling anger at your coworker because you are attached to certain outcomes in your career.

01   Feel that feeling.

Even if it's unpleasant, like sadness, boredom, anger, or hurt. Be gently present to it. Breathe the feeling in and then out. Don't run from it. Let it come to you and roll over you like a wave.

02   Offer your feeling to God in prayer and release it back to him.

You can use words or not, but just surrender that feeling back to God for him to do with as he pleases.

03   Finally, wait for God to speak to you.

See if a word or phrase or image or line from Scripture comes to mind as God's word to *you*. Write it down, and go about your day.

Reach Exercise

SESSION 02: REST

We all learn differently. Some of us prefer reading, others listening, and others doing. If you'd like to go deeper, choose what resonates with you and give it a try! Even if you don't try a Reach Exercise, remember to journal in the Sabbath Reflection section on page 52 before your next session as a group.

Reading

Read Part 01 of *Sabbath* by Dan Allender (pp. 35–97).

Podcast

Listen to Episode 02 of the Sabbath series from the *Rule of Life* podcast by Practicing the Way.

Exercise: A digital Sabbath

Turn off all your devices, including your phone, for a full 24 hours, or at least for a good portion of your Sabbath (such as from your evening Sabbath meal until noon the following day).

We recommend you literally put your phone and devices away, out of sight, in order to minimize the temptation to power back on.

This exercise will be hard at first, as your body goes through neurobiological withdrawals. You may even feel phantom phone vibrations in your pocket throughout the day. But if you stick with it, these mildly painful symptoms eventually go away and are replaced by an incredibly freeing sense of peace and presence to God and the Sabbath day.

NOTES

Sabbath Reflection

SESSION 02: REST

In between your Sabbath and your next time together with the group for Session 03, take 10 minutes to journal your answers to the following three questions.

Note: Be as specific as possible as you write. Bullet points are fine, but if you write your insights out in narrative form, your brain will be able to process them in a more lasting way.

01 Where did I feel resistance?

02 Where did I feel delight?

03 Where did I most experience God's nearness?

Delight

SESSION 03

Overview

Jesus said plainly, "In this world you will have trouble,"* but he also said his desire for his disciples was "that my joy may be in you and that your joy may be complete."** Sorrow is inevitable in this life, but joy is not. In the Way of Jesus, joy is a gift, but it's one that must be chosen and cultivated, day after day, as an act of apprenticeship to our joyful God.

Previous generations often thought of the Sabbath as a somber, serious day full of religious duty and legalistic rules. Today, many people think of it as a day to chill, relax, or sleep. Both generations miss the essential truth— the Sabbath is designed by God as a day to give yourself fully to delight in God's world, in your life in it, and ultimately in God himself.

In Session 03, we experiment with the Sabbath feast and how to spend an entire day in joy.

---

* John 16v33.

** John 15v11.

Notes

As you watch the teaching as a group, feel free to use this page for notes. What stands out to you? What's going through your brain or body right now?

Discussion Questions

Now it's time to pause the video to reflect on the teaching. Circle up in your small group and have a conversation about the following questions:

01   Does joy come naturally to you? Or is it more of a struggle for your personality?

02   What did you think of Marva J. Dawn's claim that "Americans do not know how to feast because they do not know how to fast"?* In what ways would the rest of your week need to change to set apart the Sabbath as a special day of delight?

03   Are you in a season of joy or sorrow or both? What does Sabbath keeping feel like for you at this moment in your life?

---

* Marva J. Dawn, *Keeping the Sabbath Wholly* (Grand Rapids, Mich: Eerdmans, 1989), 186.

Practice

SESSION 03: DELIGHT

Routine can help us grow in our practice and our joy. Consider how the Spirit is inviting you to practice this routine before the next session.

This session we have two very simple and very fun exercises for you.

01   Plan a Sabbath feast!

Ideally, do this together with the people around you, such as your small group or your family. Whether it's 20 people for a giant cookout in the backyard or just one or two close friends going out to dinner, plan a meal together. Cook or order your favorite foods. Make sure there's dessert. If you drink wine, save your best bottle for this meal.

Don't forget, this is an incredible chance to practice hospitality. If you have a home or apartment, host. If you know how to cook, use your skills. If you know people who don't have community or family, bring them in. Reach across the lines that divide our society—socioeconomics, race, politics, etc. Jesus' dream is for our dining room tables to look as diverse and beautiful as the kingdom of God, where every tribe, tongue, and nation are on display.

You can do this to begin your Sabbath if you start at night (as we do), to end it, or just to gather after church on Sunday.

We recommend you follow a basic Sabbath ritual:

01   Light two candles.

02   Read a psalm or liturgy, like the ones you'll find in the *Sabbath Meditations* companion book from Practicing the Way.

03 Bless the kids if they are there; bless one another.

04 Pray.

05 Feast.

06 Share highlights of the week.

07 Share what you are grateful for, or try our practice of *Dayenu*: "It would have been enough, but . . ."

08 And then just celebrate life together.

Write down a specific plan that would be life-giving for you.

02 Pleasure stacking

On the following page, make a list of activities that cause you delight and joy, and plan to do one to three of them during your Sabbath.

Here are a few ideas:

01   Make pancakes.

02   Open a good bottle of wine.

03   Have a dance party.

04   Play music.

05   Get coffee with your best friend.

06   Make love to your spouse.

07   Take a walk.

08   Nap.

09   Eat delicious food.

10   Do your nails or favorite self-care activity.

11   Go fishing or surfing or swimming.

12   Be in nature.

13   Watch the sun rise or set.

14   Make a fire.

15   Read fiction or poetry.

16   Sing.

17   Go to an art museum.

18   Go on a picnic in a beautiful park.

19   Play a game.

20   Call a friend or family member who lives far away.

Be as creative and thoughtful as you can.

List your activities.

Reach Exercise

SESSION 03: DELIGHT

We all learn differently. Some of us prefer reading, others listening, and others doing. If you'd like to go deeper, choose what resonates with you and give it a try! Even if you don't try a Reach Exercise, remember to journal in the Sabbath Reflection section on page 66 before your next session as a group.

Reading

Read Part 02 of *Sabbath* by Dan Allender (pp. 101–145).

Podcast

Listen to Episode 03 of the Sabbath series from the *Rule of Life* podcast by Practicing the Way.

Exercise: The Sabbath box

- Find a lidded container about the size of a file box or Bankers Box.

- Right before you begin your Sabbath, put in the box anything that would keep you from Sabbath delight—your phone, laptop, car keys, wallet, etc.

- Take a moment (ideally with your Sabbath meal community), and write out any anxieties, sorrows, or unfinished tasks from the previous session (there are *always* things we ran out of time to get done).

- Say a brief prayer giving it all over to God's care, and then put the box away for your Sabbath as an embodied act of trust in God.

- From there, begin your Sabbath meal or beginning ritual.

NOTES

Sabbath Reflection

SESSION 03: DELIGHT

In between your Sabbath and your next time together with the group for Session 04, take 10 minutes to journal your answers to the following three questions.

Note: Be as specific as possible as you write. Bullet points are fine, but if you write your insights out in narrative form, your brain will be able to process them in a more lasting way.

01 **Where did I feel resistance?**

02 **Where did I feel delight?**

03 **Where did I most experience God's nearness?**

Worship

SESSION 04

Overview

For many Western Christians, Sunday has become what Eugene Peterson called a "bastard Sabbath"—the illegitimate offspring of the Sabbath and a secular day off.*

Whether you practice Sabbath on Sunday, Saturday, or another day of the week, it's essential to remember God commands us to "remember the Sabbath day by keeping it holy."** To keep it "holy" means to sanctify it, set it apart, and dedicate it to God for his special purposes. Sabbath isn't just a day to sleep in, relax, and do whatever brings you joy (it *is*, but it's *more*); it's a day to worship. To reorient your entire life back to its center in God.

In our final session of Sabbath, we elevate the Sabbath from a restful, joyful day off to a holy day of worship and delight in God himself.

---

* Eugene H. Peterson, "The Good-for-Nothing Sabbath," *Christianity Today*, April 4, 1994, www.christianitytoday.com/1994/04/good-for-nothing-sabbath/.

** Exodus 20v8.

Notes

As you watch the teaching as a group, feel free to use this page for notes. What stands out or resonates with you?

Discussion Questions

Now it's time to pause the video to reflect on the teaching in your small groups. Here are some questions to give shape to your discussion:

01 In what ways is it easy for your practice of Sabbath to become "sabbish," more of a day off than a day of worship?

02 How do you enjoy God? What practices, disciplines, or activities bring you genuine joy in God?

03 What "false gods" are you tempted to worship that, while they may be very good things (or not), pull you away from your holy center in God?

Practice

SESSION 04: WORSHIP

The practice of Sabbath can slowly change the trajectory of your entire life! Consider how the Spirit is working in you and your community to invite you into deeper worship.

For our final session, we have two exercises for you.

01 Practice a light and life-giving version of what the ancients called "fixed-hour prayer"

All that means is you pause two to three times during your 24-hour Sabbath to pray. Please note, this is not a time for intercessory prayer when you ask God to move in the world. The goal is to develop a ritual of reorientation. In fact, in Orthodox Judaism, intercessory prayer is forbidden on the Sabbath because it's a form of work. Prayer in the wider sense is a reorientation of your heart to God in wonder and awe. One understanding of prayer is coming to rest in God's goodness. Two to three times this Sabbath, rest in God's goodness.

The most ancient and, for many people, the most helpful way to do this is by praying a psalm, such as Psalm 23, 37, 103, or 105.

You can also do this by listening to worship music or praying with a friend or going on a walk in nature—the options are endless.

The end goal is to spend as much of the Sabbath as you possibly can in conscious communion with God, just receiving his love for you and giving back your love for him.

Jot down your plan here.

02 Identify two to three practices by which you enjoy God, and do them

It's key to discover what the spiritual writer Gary Thomas calls your "sacred pathway"—the way you are uniquely wired to enjoy God.

For you this could be time alone in stillness, or it could be throwing a raucous party with your community. It could be walking in nature or reading a novel by the fire. It could be an emotional experience, or it could be the intellectual study of theology, philosophy, or quantum physics. It could be a sensory act such as walking, fishing, or bird-watching.

As you discern which activities are a good fit for your Sabbath Practice, it can be difficult to know whether certain things are appropriate. One simple rubric is to filter every potential activity through the four movements of Sabbath:

01 **Stop** — *Is this ceasing what I do on normal workdays?* For example, if you work as a mechanic but you really enjoy gardening, even though it can be a bit physical, that may be a beautiful Sabbath activity for you. But if you're a landscaper, it's likely not the best fit for your Sabbath Practice.

02 **Rest** — *Is this restful? Does it refill my soul with new energy emotionally, intellectually, physically, spiritually?* Things like watching TV may give us a welcome break, but we seldom feel new energy for life when we're done.

03 **Delight** — *Does this activity bring me deep, visceral joy in God? Do I find myself naturally happy and grateful and connected to God as I do it?*

04 **Worship** — *Does this activity connect me more deeply to God and his goodness and beauty? Do I find myself coming alive to the wonder of his nature and spontaneously bursting into praise?*

However you enjoy God and whatever the practices you love, do a few of them this coming Sabbath.

The point of both these exercises is to live in what Jesus called "abiding"— not only all Sabbath long but also all week long.

What two to three practices might the Spirit be inviting you into?

Reach Exercise

SESSION 04: WORSHIP

We all learn differently. Some of us prefer reading, others listening, and others doing. If you'd like to go deeper, choose what resonates with you and give it a try! Even if you don't try a Reach Exercise, remember to journal in the Sabbath Reflection section on page 80 before your next session as a group.

Reading

Read Part 03 and the conclusion of *Sabbath* by Dan Allender (pp. 149–194).

Podcast

Listen to Episode 04 of the Sabbath series from the *Rule of Life* podcast by Practicing the Way.

Exercise: Silence and solitude

Our final Reach Exercise is to spend a portion of your Sabbath in the quiet with God. There is a special kind of stillness that comes on the Sabbath when our relationship to time is unhurried and we savor more than we stress. See if you can tap into that Sabbath time and give it back to God in loving worship.

To do this, we recommend you find a quiet, distraction-free time and place. For many, first thing in the morning is the ideal time, but do whatever works best for your life.

For couples with younger children, consider breaking the day into thirds— a third spent all together in delight, a third for one parent to go be alone to rest and pray while the other plays with the children, and a third where the parents swap places.

Spend your time in silence and solitude reading Scripture, journaling, walking in nature, or just napping and prayerfully resting in God—whatever your pathway is to God's peace and presence.

Sabbath Reflection

SESSION 04: WORSHIP

After your Sabbath, take 10 minutes to journal your answers to the following three questions.

Note: Be as specific as possible as you write. Bullet points are fine, but if you write your insights out in narrative form, your brain will be able to process them in a more lasting way.

---

01 Where did I feel resistance?

---

02 Where did I feel delight?

---

03 Where did I most experience God's nearness?

Continue to share what you are learning about God, Sabbath, and your spiritual journey with a close friend or community member.

NOTES

Keep Going

Recommended Exercises to Continue the Journey

Allow yourself to engage in a consistent rhythm of Sabbath so that this Practice can become a part of you. This four-session Practice is designed to be a starting point on a lifelong journey. It's meant to be integrated into your Rule of Life for you to come back to over and over. It takes most people years, if not decades, to really learn to sabbath as God intended, but the process will be filled with rest, delight, and worship. Through it, may you truly experience life.

Where you go from here is entirely up to you, but if you decide to integrate Sabbath into your weekly rhythm, here are some next steps to continue your practice:

Recommended reading

01   *Keeping the Sabbath Wholly* by Marva J. Dawn

02   *The Sabbath* by Abraham Joshua Heschel

03   *Subversive Sabbath* by A.J. Swoboda

04   *The Ruthless Elimination of Hurry* by John Mark Comer

Recommended exercises

01   Build a Sabbath Practice with all 12 traditional Sabbath activities

Consider adding one new activity at your own pace—per week or month or season. Don't rush this; take your time and enjoy yourself.

01   Lighting the candles

02   Blessing the children

03   Eating a Sabbath meal

04   Expressing gratitude

05   Singing

06   Worshipping with your church

07   Walking

08   Napping

09   Making love to your spouse

10   Reading, especially Scripture

11   Spending time alone with God

12   Spending time with family and friends in conversation and celebration

Try all of them and keep any that you find helpful.

Note: Find a way to do each of these that are a good fit for you—your personality, stage of life, spiritual temperament, etc.

02 Go on a weekend retreat

Find a monastery, retreat center, rural hotel, or vacation home. Book a few days by yourself (or with a few close friends or community members) for an extended Sabbath, to stop, rest, delight, and worship. The longer we give ourselves to rest, the more space it opens up in us for healing and renewal.

03 Take a weeklong (or longer) Sabbath vacation

Overwhelming numbers of Americans don't take more than seven days of vacation a year. And across the Western world, many people's "vacations" are exactly what they sound like—an attempt to "vacate" their lives. These are often crammed full of activities that they pay for instead of getting paid to do. For this reason, many people come home from their vacations even more exhausted, behind, and in debt than when they began.

There is another way. While vacations to play, travel, and experience can be wonderful and life-giving, there is also a place for time off work for an extended Sabbath. In the Torah, the Sabbath was every seventh day, but three times a year all Israel would take an entire week off work to rest, worship, and feast together before God. This ancient pattern still holds wisdom for the modern world.

- Find a place that is as restful as possible. If you can afford it or have access, go to the beach or the mountains or somewhere out of the way. If not, intentionally create a restful space for yourself wherever you are.

- Bring your community with you, even if it's just your family or a few of your closest confidants.

- Do what you do on Sabbath but for seven days. Turn off your phone, cease all work, and sleep, rest, enjoy margin, celebrate, eat, dance, talk, laugh, and—above all—worship God.

The Practices

Information alone isn't enough to produce transformation.

By adopting not just the teaching but the practices from Jesus' own life, we open up our entire beings to God and allow him to transform us into people of love.

Our nine core Practices work together to form a Rule of Life for the modern era.

Sabbath	Prayer	Fasting
Solitude	Generosity	Scripture
Community	Service	Witness

WHAT'S INCLUDED FOR EACH PRACTICE

Four Sessions
Each session includes teaching, guided discussion, and weekly exercises to integrate the Practice into daily life.

Companion Guide
A detailed Guide provides question prompts, session-by-session exercises, and space to write and reflect.

Recommended Resources
Additional recommended readings and podcasts offer a way to get the most out of the Practice.

The Practicing the Way Course

An eight-session primer on spiritual formation

Two thousand years ago, Jesus said to his disciples, "Follow me." But what does it mean for us to follow Jesus today?

The Practicing the Way Course is an on-ramp to spiritual formation, exploring what it means to follow Jesus and laying the foundation for a life of apprenticeship to him.

WHAT'S INCLUDED

Eight Sessions

John Mark and other voices teaching on apprenticing under Jesus, spiritual formation, healing from sin, meeting God in pain, crafting a Rule of Life, living in community, and more

Exercises

Weekly practices and exercises to help integrate what you've learned into your everyday life

Guided Conversation

Prompts to reflect on your experience and process honestly in community

Companion Guide

A detailed workbook with exercises, space to write and reflect, and suggestions for supplemental resources

The **Practicing the Way** Course

The Circle

Practicing the Way is a nonprofit that develops spiritual formation resources for churches and small groups learning how to become apprentices in the Way of Jesus.

We believe one of the greatest needs of our time is for people to discover how to become lifelong disciples of Jesus. To that end, we help people learn how to be with Jesus, become like him, and do as he did, through the practices and rhythms he and his earliest followers lived by.

All of our downloadable ministry resources are available at no cost, thanks to the generosity of The Circle and other givers from around the world who partner with us to see formation integrated into the church at large.

To learn more or join us, visit practicingtheway.org/give.

To inquire about ordering this Companion Guide in bulk quantities for your church, small group, or staff, contact churches@penguinrandomhouse.com.